CONTENTS

CHAPTER THREE Library Publications   *20*

PAULA BANKS

CHAPTER FOUR Planning Special Events   *31*

DEBORA MESKAUSKAS

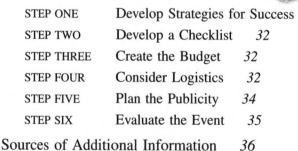

FIGURES

Note: Some of the layout examples are slightly reduced to fit the page. Measurements are not exact, but proportions are correct.

ACKNOWLEDGMENTS

The authors of these chapters and the editor wish to acknowledge the contributions of the LAMA PRS Publications Committee members who served on the committee while this publication was in progress.

Paula Banks—Medina County District Library (Ohio)

Dorothy E. Christiansen—University of Albany,
  State University of New York

Patricia E. Dick—Fort Stockton Public Library (Texas)

Denise Forro—Michigan State University

Ann Hamilton—Georgia Southern University

Rashelle S. Karp—Clarion University of Pennsylvania

Debora Meskauskas—Arlington Heights Memorial Library (Illinois)

Beth K. Steele—Homewood (Alabama)

INTRODUCTION

WILLIAM BUCHANAN

For many, the phrase "public relations" conjures up images of Madison Avenue executives who polish and promote a product beyond recognition. The modus operandi of such executives is the "blitz campaign," in which the product is showcased in a star-studded series of high-profile publicity "splashes."

This is *not* the stuff of which library public relations campaigns are made. To be sure, librarians can, should, and, in fact, do develop programming around special events that are highly publicized. But the purpose of a library's public relations program is not the quick-sell, publicity-at-any-price mentality.

The purpose of library public relations is to develop ongoing programs of contact between the librarians and the population groups that they serve.

All libraries can benefit from a public that is informed about, supportive of, and involved in the library's operations. Why can libraries benefit from such programs? And, equally important, why should you, the beleaguered librarian, library paraprofessional, or library volunteer, add one more job to your growing list of duties?

The answer to these questions is, in part, in the definition of the institution itself: libraries are institutions designed for use. In order to be used, libraries must be familiar to user groups. A public relations program allows the library staff to maintain positive, supportive communications with the library's public, including current and potential users. A public relations program provides a systematic, ongoing means by which library staff can communicate with, report to, and receive feedback from active and potential user groups.

As libraries change, evolve, and expand their services, they continuously develop the potential for attracting new clientele and providing more and better services for existing clientele. This potential is most likely to be fully realized when the clientele that can benefit from the library's services is kept informed about what is available. Public relations efforts can impact the use of new services in an often dramatic way. Take, for instance, the decision by some public librarians to add videotapes to their collections. For many libraries, announcements in the local press of the availability of feature-length videotapes resulted in dramatic increases in newly registered patrons and circulation statistics. Or take the case of the academic library that announced on the campus radio station that the library could provide Internet access to a variety of full-text journal articles. Immediately, traffic into the library increased, as did talk on campus about the library's services. However, the real work of public relations is less glamorous and dramatic than the occasional announcement of video collections or Internet access; it is an ongoing planned program of dissemination of information to the public designed to maintain a consistent level of awareness of what the library is, what it is doing, and how the public can benefit from and contribute to it.

Public relations can be accomplished through exhibits and displays in the library, special events for community groups, newsletters and other ongoing library-produced publications, newspaper items (both news items and ongoing feature columns), public service announcements (over electronic news outlets, radio, and television), and in a variety of other ways. It is accomplished by librarians, library paraprofessionals, and library volunteers.

This book is aimed at librarians, library paraprofessionals, and library volunteers who would like to create a program of public relations for their libraries or who would like to improve an existing program of public relations. Each chapter is written for practitioners or would-be practitioners of public relations. Taken together, the chapters provide a wealth of "how-to" advice for mounting and maintaining an effective library public relations program.

News Releases, Photo Releases, Public Service Announcements

L ibraries are not just quiet places to read. Programs, discussion groups, book sales, storyhours, and a variety of other types of events are being held in libraries. One of the best ways to let the public know what programs and events are available to them is to publicize the events in the local media—newspapers, radios and television stations.

NEWS RELEASES

What Is a News Release?

A news release is a short written statement which is sent to the media for publication. News releases are written to notify the public that something significant has just occurred or is about to occur.

News releases:

- Announce new programs or services at the library

- Report on the progress and success of a program or service offered at the library

- Provide new information about existing programs and services offered at the library

- Announce special events, seasonal programs, or meetings at the library

- Inform the public about positions or policies adopted by the library

- Communicate statements made by officers or directors of the library on topics of interest to the community

- Introduce new library staff to the community

- Describe materials that have been added to the library's collections

Writing News Releases

All news releases must include information on (1) whom the announcement is about; (2) what the announcement is about; (3) where the event is taking place; (4) when the event is taking place; and (5) why the public may be interested in what is being announced.

Who   Who is presenting the program? Who was recently hired? Who has approved the policy? Who has written the new materials added to the library's collection?

What   Is the announcement about a meeting, a new program or service, new books, policy statements, or new hires?

When   What is the exact time that an event will or did take place: "Thursday, January 11, at 10:00 a.m."

Where   What is the exact place that an event will or did take place: "Community room of the Clarion Free Public Library, 1234 Maple Street, Clarion, Penn."

Why   Why should people be interested in the announced event: "Anyone who has ever wanted to use a word processing program will want to attend this workshop on Word Perfect 6.1."

General Do's and Don'ts of News Releases

Do hand deliver your news release if possible.

Do clearly indicate why your news release is timely and newsworthy.

Do identify your library fully.

Do identify if the announced event is free and open to the public.

Do cover all the facts. Assume that the readers have no background information on the subject of your news release.

Do refer to women and men in the same way. Use first names, middle initials, and last names for the first reference to a person. Subsequent references should use just the last name.

Do check every news release carefully to ensure that all the information is complete and accurate.

Do verify spellings of all names.

Don't use initials, abbreviations, or acronyms to refer to your library or library programs.

Don't use technical terms or library jargon. News release copy should be written at a junior high school reading level.

Don't ever spell a person's name wrong.

Don't editorialize. If you must convey subjective ideas, use direct quotes. Quotes add life to news release copy and allow you to mention the names of people.

Don't use superlatives in describing your library, its services, or its programs.

What Does a News Release Look Like?

A news release must be structured so that the most important part comes first. The most important part of a news release is usually any information which relates to the purpose of the news release (e.g., "children's story hour scheduled for next month," or "you can return your overdue books without paying any overdue fines"). After the first piece of information, details should be added in descending order of importance, with the least important information coming last. This is called an *inverted pyramid* style of writing.

Following are some general guidelines about the contents and appearance of a news release:

- Send the news release on library letterhead or on plain paper, but, whichever is used, clearly identify the library.

- Begin each news release with the name and address of the person to whom it is being sent. This information should be in the upper left hand corner of the release.

- List the name of the person to be contacted if the newspaper needs more information before printing the news release. The contact's name and telephone number should go in the upper left corner of the release, directly under the name and address of the person to whom the release is being sent. If there is a contact person for questions from the general public, this name and number (or address) should be within the body of the news release.

- Indicate when the information in the news release may be released. This should be clearly indicated in the upper left corner of the release, just above the name of the person to whom questions should be addressed (e.g., "FOR RELEASE: FRIDAY, JUNE 5"; or "FOR IMMEDIATE RELEASE").

- Type a headline (subject heading) for the release in capital letters at the beginning of the text.

- Doublespace the news release.

- Use only one side of the paper.

- Keep the release short. There are no hard and fast rules about the length of a release, but a length of one or two doublespaced pages is best.

- When a news release continues on to a second page, don't end the first page in the middle of a paragraph. If the entire paragraph does not fit at the end of the page, start the paragraph at the beginning of the second page.

- When a news release has two pages, type "MORE" at the bottom of the first page; type "Page 2" and the subject heading of the release at the top of the second page.

- End the news release with "###" or "-30-". To an editor or a typesetter, this indicates the end of a news item.

Figure 1.1 is a sample news release that should help to put all of the previous points into perspective.

PHOTO RELEASES

When important news events occur, newspapers often send a staff photographer to cover them. Newspapers are especially interested in acquiring unusual picture ideas to illustrate stories.

Here are some suggestions regarding photo releases:

- Establish a rapport with the photographers or photo editors of the local newspapers in order to develop a routine where a photographer is often sent to cover the events that the librarians identify as newsworthy.

- If a photographer is sent to cover a library event, make suggestions regarding pictures that are creative, rather than pictures that are routine. For example, many newspapers will not photograph presentations of checks, handshaking, or signings of proclamations. However, they might photograph a group of children using the new reading room which was funded by one person's generosity, or they might photograph the line of people waiting to get into the library after the passing of a local referendum which allowed the public library to remain open on Sunday.

- Before the photographer arrives, be sure that all the people and props are ready.

- Provide the photographer with a "cut line" (caption) for the picture which identifies all of the people (names spelled correctly) and describes the event.

- If a press photographer is not able to come to the library to cover an event, offer to send people to the newspaper office for a staged "photo opportunity."

- If a press photographer cannot cover the library event, and the people involved cannot get to the newspaper office, you can take your own black and white picture. However, be aware that most newspaper policies state that photos will not be returned.

FIGURE 1.1 **News Release Sample**

M.K. Blackley, City Editor, Gazette

123 Elm Street

Anytown, OH 44220

FOR IMMEDIATE RELEASE

CONTACT: Mary Jones, 226-2467

Public Information Officer

Anytown Public Library

SOCKS DISAPPEARING AT THE LIBRARY!

The children's room at the Wonderful Library has a new addition—a very large sock-eating plant. The sock-eating plant is there to promote the visit of author Nancy McArthur.

McArthur will be in the children's room of Anytown Public Library, 1234 Maple Street, on Thursday, November 10. She will give a booktalk featuring her most recent book, The Secret of the Plant that Ate Dirty Socks, at 10:00 a.m. McArthur will be available until noon for signing books. You'll enjoy visiting with this humorous and imaginative author. The Secret of the Plant That Ate Dirty Socks continues the saga of two brothers, one messy, the other a neatness nut, and their weird but lovable pet plant.

This sequel continues the hilarious adventures begun in the bestsellers, The Plant That Ate Dirty Socks, The Return of the Plant That Ate Dirty Socks, and The Escape of the Plant That Ate Dirty Socks.

Exie Exlibris, Children's Librarian, says, "This is a program you won't want to miss. McArthur will knock your socks off."

The Village Booksmith will have books available for purchase and autographs. The program is sponsored by the Friends of the Anytown Public Library, and is free and open to the public.

###

PUBLIC SERVICE ANNOUNCEMENTS (PSAs)

What Are PSAs?

PSAs are short messages about nonprofit organizations that are broadcast over the radio or television at no charge. Although PSAs are usually used to motivate people to do something, they cannot be commercial in nature. For example, a PSA might solicit volunteers for a special program, or it might be aimed at getting patrons to call the library's new telephone information reference service. However, it cannot be directed at advertising a for-profit business, nor can it include the names of any corporate sponsors for a library's program.

PSAs can be broadcast over the radio, television, or computer networks.

- If radio is used, PSAs are either read live by the station announcer or they can be prerecorded.

- If television is used, you will want to explore which cable channels are available for local access by nonprofit groups. This access will vary from town to town and from state to state. The type of access that a library might receive could range from minimal broadcast time, to free-of-charge use of studios and equipment. Occasionally, cable companies will also contribute their own staff to help with the production of a PSA.

- If a computer network is used, electronic bulletin boards should be chosen to target appropriate audiences.

Creating PSAs

The most important thing to remember as you write a PSA for radio is that you are writing for people's ears, not for their eyes. The broadcast audience cannot reread a sentence if it is not clear, and, if parts of the PSA are boring, the audience cannot skim over the boring parts in order to get to the important parts. If the message is boring, broadcast audiences will "tune out" and disregard it. Following are some general suggestions for writing a PSA:

- Write as you would speak.

- Keep the sentence structure simple. For example, this is a poor sentence for a PSA: "The library's literacy series, sponsored by Laubach Literacy Council, and focused on the needs of adults who have trouble reading, encourages all interested adults to apply." This is better: "The library encourages adults with reading difficulties to apply for the library's literacy series, sponsored by Laubach Literacy Council."

- Attribute direct quotes at the beginning of a sentence. For example, "Director Johnson says, 'The library is the center of town activity.'"

- Provide a pronunciation key for any words or names in a PSA that might be difficult to pronounce. For example, "Trustee Earl Guogin (pronounced Jo-jin), called . . ."

- Make your copy as clear and concise as possible so that the broadcast station does not have to edit it. This will avoid any editing changes that inadvertently change the meaning of your PSA.

- If you are given a time limit for a PSA (e.g., 30 seconds), make sure that the copy you prepare does not go over the time limit when it is read. In determining how much to put into the PSA, remember that less is better than too much. If a PSA has too much content, the broadcast audience will be confused. One way to say less but still allow a lot of information to be presented is to end the PSA with a telephone number or address for more information.

- PSAs should run 10, 20, 30, or 60 seconds. The shorter ones generally have more chance of being used, so you will want to know in advance what a station's policies and formats allow. A good rule of thumb is to allow about two and a half regular length words to each second. So:

  25 words will take 10 seconds to say

  50 words will take 20 seconds to say

  75 words will take 30 seconds to say

  150 words will take 60 seconds to say

  If some of the words are longer, you should allow a little more time. Also, each digit of a telephone number should be counted as a separate word.

- Test the length of a PSA by timing it as you read it out loud.

Typing and Submitting PSAs

A PSA should be prepared in the most appealing manner possible. Things to consider include:

- Identify the PSA as a Public Service Announcement in the upper left hand corner.

- Identify the library directly under the PSA identification.

- Provide a contact person in case the broadcaster needs more information. The contact identification should be placed directly under the library identification.

- Include an indication of the PSA's length.

- Indicate the dates for which the announcement is in effect. Although you will determine a date range for the release of a PSA, you will not be able to dictate the times that a PSA will be aired. If it is accepted, the public service director will put your PSA into a rotation along with other announcements that get made.

- For radio PSAs, use triple spacing for the text, use all capital letters, and only include one announcement per page.

- For radio PSAs, separate phrases in the copy with three dots (. . .) according to what can comfortably be read in one breath. The breaks allow the broadcaster to read the announcement more smoothly.

- For television PSAs, a 3/4 inch video tape is preferred.

- Send the PSA to the *public service director* at the broadcast station as far in advance as possible.

- Send a cover letter with the PSA which explains the purpose of the announcement and any other pertinent information.

Figure 1.2 is an example of a radio PSA.

EVALUATION OF NEWS RELEASES, PHOTO RELEASES, AND PSAs

Keep copies of the published releases and photos. Determine which papers most consistently publish library information and photographs.

One way to evaluate your success with this method of publicity is to count the number of news releases and photographs published in the newspaper and to keep count of the number of PSAs broadcast. However, do not judge your success based only on this data because too often a "soft news story" will be bumped for a world or local event. Newspapers can only print

FIGURE 1.2 **Sample PSA**

Public Service Announcement
Wonderful Public Library

From: Mary Jones
        Public Information Officer
        Wonderful District Public Library
        789-1234

                                    10 seconds
                                    For use through September 1993

YOU CAN RESERVE BOOKS FROM THE WONDERFUL PUBLIC LIBRARY . . .

ON YOUR HOME COMPUTER! . . .

CALL SEVEN-EIGHT-NINE . . . ONE-TWO-THREE-FOUR . . .

TO LEARN THE SECRET.

in the space they have available. If no news releases have been published, ask for an interview with the appropriate editor to discuss how publicity about library events could be included in the local news section.

Keep track informally by asking patrons where they heard about the program/event.

SOURCES OF ADDITIONAL INFORMATION

Leerburger, Benedict A. *Promoting and Marketing the Library.* Boston: G.K. Hall, 1989.

Leerburger has been on the Board of Trustees for two different public libraries. This updated version of his first book (*Marketing the Library.* White Plains, NY: Knowledge Industry Publications, 1982) provides a brief history of libraries and an introduction to the philosophical foundations for marketing in libraries. The chapters on press releases are especially helpful, as are the chapters on promoting academic and special libraries, and working with friends groups. Leerburger's thesis is that in order for libraries to survive budget cuts and higher operating costs, librarians must market their services.

Roberts, Anne F. and Susan Griswold Blandy. *Public Relations for Librarians.* Englewood, CO: Libraries Unlimited, 1989.

Divided into two parts, this excellent primer first discusses public relations (what it is and how it works in libraries) and then discusses public relations opportunities in all types of libraries.

Tuggle, Ann Montgomery and Dawn Hansen Heller. *Grand Schemes and Nitty Gritty Details: Library PR That Works.* Littleton, CO: Libraries Unlimited, 1987.

Part one of this book illustrates eight different attributes of John Cotton Dana winners. Part two uses examples from various libraries as well as descriptions to explain the "how to" of developing a successful public relations program.

Exhibits

**WHAT ARE
EXHIBITS?**

Exhibits are displays of items which increase a library's visibility and inform library users about a library's collections and services. An exhibits program includes all of the steps that go into creating an exhibit or group of exhibits. Developing and soliciting exhibits provide opportunities for a library to develop partnerships with its communities, thereby increasing a library's base of local support and making people more aware of the library.

**CREATING AN
EXHIBITS PROGRAM**

In order to mount a successful exhibits program, the following steps should be taken:

STEP ONE

Put Someone in Charge

A successful exhibits program will ideally be managed from start to finish by the same person or group of people. This focus will help to ensure that exhibits and displays consistently meet standards for quality, and will also help to avoid confusion when an external group requests space in the library for an exhibit.

STEP TWO

Develop an Exhibits Program Policy

An Exhibits Program Policy (see Figure 2.1) is an official statement which (1) identifies the types of exhibits which can be mounted in the library; (2) indicates how individuals or groups can apply to use exhibit space; and (3) provides criteria which will be used to approve or reject an exhibit application. Librarians developing an Exhibits Program Policy

FIGURE 2.1   Library Exhibits Policy

Exhibits Policy
Wonderful Public Library

The library makes exhibit cases and other display areas available for display of materials which support the institution's programs and services. Of special interest to the library are exhibits which promote the library's collections, services, and programs. Exhibits should contribute positively to the library's environment, highlight collection strengths, publicize the resources and services of the library, enrich the life of the community, and be a means of strengthening partnerships between the library and its community.

EXHIBITS COORDINATOR

The Exhibits Coordinator is responsible for exhibits mounted in the library.
   The responsibilities of the Exhibits Coordinator are:

- to develop and execute an annual plan of exhibits.

- to review incoming requests for mounting an exhibit.

- to mount exhibits.

- to assist exhibitors who wish to mount exhibits.

CRITERIA FOR EXHIBITS

Exhibits accepted for display in the library's exhibit and display areas should satisfy the following criteria:

- relate to the mission of the library and its parent organization;

- be sponsored by the library or an approved individual, organization, or agency;

- be fair and equitable concerning issues of potential controversy;

- be aesthetically pleasing;

- display materials relevant to the theme of the exhibit;

- promote the materials, services, and functions of the library;

- facilitate cooperative relations between the library and the community it serves.

PROCEDURES

- An application form should be obtained from the Exhibits Coordinator or the library's administrative office. The form should be submitted at least three months in advance of the proposed date of the requested exhibit.

- The application form should be returned to the Exhibits Coordinator or the library's administrative office. If delivered to the office, it will be forwarded to the Exhibits Coordinator, who will respond to the person requesting permission to mount an exhibit.

- The Exhibits Coordinator will review all applications and make a decision to approve or reject the application.

(continued)

- The Exhibits Coordinator will assess all applications on the basis of the criteria listed above. Applicants will be informed by the Exhibits Coordinator of the status (approval/rejection) of their applications. Successful applicants will be provided with a confirmed time and place for the proposed exhibit.

- Exhibits must be ready for installation and must include all necessary identifying labels. Unless otherwise indicated, it is the responsibility of the exhibitor to dismantle the exhibit after the display period is completed.

- Insurance for items of value used in exhibits and not owned by the library is the responsibility of the donor of the item(s).

- Circulation of items: All items owned by the library and borrowed from library collections for display purposes must be charged out to EXHIBIT according to established procedures. Items on exhibit are subject to recall compliances.

should refer to the principles set forth in the American Library Association's "EXHIBIT SPACES AND BULLETIN BOARDS: An Interpretation of the LIBRARY BILL OF RIGHTS" (Adopted July 2, 1991, by the American Library Association Council). The parts of an exhibit program policy usually include the sections described below:

Goals And Objectives

This section describes the goals and objectives for the exhibits program. Specifically, what does the organization hope to achieve from the exhibits program? Why is it important for the library to have an exhibits program? And what, in the end, will the benefits be?

Exhibits Coordinator

This part of the policy identifies the staff who will be responsible for the program. It also identifies the coordinator's responsibilities.

Criteria

This portion of the policy defines who can mount exhibits in library exhibit space, for what purpose, and how the exhibit materials should be presented. It also describes the criteria that are used to accept or reject an exhibit application.

Procedures

This portion of the exhibits policy:

1. Informs all potential exhibitors of the procedures involved in applying for exhibit space. Exhibit applications (see Figure 2.2) should supply information regarding the nature and purpose of the exhibit, when the exhibit is to be mounted, how long it will be left in the library, and where it should be placed in the library.

FIGURE 2.2 Application for Exhibit/Display Space

Application for Exhibit/Display Space

Name: _____

Address: _____

_____

Department/Organization: _____

Telephone Number: _____

Proposed Dates for Exhibit: _____

Proposed Title of Exhibit: _____

Please describe the purpose and nature of the exhibit relating the description to the attached *Exhibits Policy* (attach to this form).

Cases requested—list preference:

Location	*Size*
_____ Library Lobby	72″ × 36″ × 9″—flat (2 cases)
_____ Library Lobby	60″ × 22″ × 9″—flat (4 cases)
_____ Library Lower Level	72″ × 45″ × 18″—upright (2 cases, 4 glass shelves per case)

Signature _____ Date _____

Please return application form to: Exhibits Coordinator, Address, Telephone number

_____

This area is for use by the Exhibits Coordinator.

Decision or Recommendation of the Exhibits Coordinator:

Signature _____ Date _____

2. Describes the review process by which applications are accepted or rejected.

3. Indicates the types of insurance and security that the library will provide for exhibits.

4. Outlines any procedures necessary for the circulation of exhibited materials.

STEP THREE
Identify Space, Equipment, Supplies, and Budgetary Needs

Space

Exhibits must be able to be seen. For example, exhibit cases and bulletin boards should be located in primary traffic flow areas but should not interfere with the traffic flow.

Informational signs must be placed at strategic locations to inform library users about exhibits at the library.

Equipment

Choose the medium for the exhibit carefully. Library supply catalogs and furniture catalogs advertise many types of *exhibit cases* (flat glass cases to upright shelved units) and *bulletin boards* (wall-mounted units to movable display panels). The choice of an exhibit case or bulletin board should be determined by (1) the available space, (2) the type of exhibit, (3) preservation considerations, (4) the budget, and (5) security (for example, lockable cases and bulletin boards are essential in unsupervised areas).

Obtain access to a microcomputer and laser printer with appropriate software for printing signs and text.

Supplies

Exhibit supplies include everything from basic office supplies (such as scissors, staples, Scotch™ tape, thumbtacks, rulers, colored paper, colored markers, and rubber cement) to "exhibit-specific" supplies such as book display stands, blocks to vary the height of displayed items, lettering templates, colored poster board, ultraviolet Plexiglass™ to protect displayed items, and colored background cloth.

In many instances, exhibit supplies are recyclable (display stands, thumbtacks). In some instances, the supplies that are available determine the type of exhibit to be mounted.

Budget

Other than staff time, the most costly part of an exhibits program is the one-time purchase of display cases, wall-mounted units, and computer equipment and software.

An annual exhibits program budget should include exhibit supplies, repairs, and, if traveling exhibits are going to be used, transportation, shipping, and other related costs. The cost of insuring exhibit materials must also be factored into the budget, unless the library's general liability policy covers these items.

STEP FOUR
Develop Security, Preservation, and Circulation Strategies

Security Strategies

Materials on exhibit (including library exhibits, loaned exhibits, and traveling exhibits) must be protected from loss or vandalism. Whenever possible, exhibits should be displayed in locked exhibit cases or locked wall cases and bulletin boards.

Preservation Strategies

Librarians must take extreme care not to display materials in ways which are harmful. For example, if the exhibit is to be up for an extended period or if it includes manuscripts or rare materials, ultraviolet Plexiglass™ should be used to protect the items from ultraviolet rays. Also, librarians should avoid placing exhibit cases in direct sunlight since sunlight fades documents and heat speeds deterioration. Finally, in order to avoid chemical reactions between display items and their mounting apparatus, librarians should use inert materials such as Plexiglass™, acrylic, and covered metal, rather than wood.

Circulation Strategies

The best evidence that an exhibits program is working might be when patrons ask to borrow books which are in the exhibit. The library's general circulation policy should include policies and procedures for the circulation of exhibit materials. Generally, a more liberal circulation policy is desirable, since the purpose of many exhibits is to increase circulation. Sometimes, it is better to loan an item from an exhibit, even if the loan results in a less aesthetically pleasing display. Often, librarians purchase duplicate copies of items on display so that the second copy can be circulated while the first copy is unavailable. Reserve lists for items can also be used.

STEP FIVE
Prepare a Schedule and Develop Presentation Guidelines

Planning effective exhibits requires consideration of community and institutional calendars in order to avoid conflicts in the scheduling of events such as a kickoff for the exhibit, or special events which utilize the exhibit. An exhibit must also be planned far enough in advance so that sufficient preparation time is allotted.

The following recommendations should be considered in designing an exhibit.

- The choice of a type of case for an exhibit depends upon the types of materials that are to be included. For example, books and artifacts are best presented in locked upright shelved cases or flat cases. In contrast, two-dimensional materials, such as posters, pictures, and brochures, are best presented on bulletin boards and panel boards.

- The individuals who prepared an exhibit should always be acknowledged somewhere in the exhibit. In some instances, an explanatory flyer, brochure, or a selected reading list can be made available near the exhibit.

- All exhibits must have a clearly stated theme or focus which is made known to viewers by a title label or a title label with a paragraph of explanation.

- Display materials must be directly related to the stated theme of an exhibit.

- The style and arrangement throughout all of the cases of an exhibit should be consistent.

- Hardware (book racks, wood and plastic elevators) should be consistent throughout an exhibit, and should be as invisible as possible to the viewer.

- Layout of exhibits should be simple in order not to draw attention away from exhibited items.

- One typeface should be used for all of the labels in an exhibit. Twelve-point typeface for text, and 14- to 16-point typeface for exhibit titles are recommended. In order to emphasize text within labels (e.g., a book title or an interesting quote), different styles within a typeface can be used (e.g., bold or italics).

- Labels should be mounted on poster board backing (one subtle color should be used throughout the exhibit) to prevent them from curling.

- Labels should be provided for each item or group of similar items to explain how they fit into the theme of the exhibit. If the exhibited item is a book and the author/title is not visible to the viewer, the author and title should be cited on a label. If the exhibit carries over into noncontiguous cases (e.g., first floor and reserve area) a label in the last contiguous case should direct viewers to the next case.

- The amount of text on each label should be consistent throughout the exhibit. As a rule of thumb, one to two lines fit comfortably on a 5″ × 2″ label; one to two paragraphs fit on a 5″ × 5″ or 7″ × 10″ label.

- To hold a book open to a particular page without impairing the visibility of the text or damaging the book, use clear Mylar™ tape. To highlight text from a book without damaging the book, use clear yellow cellophane, trimmed to fit the size of the text to be highlighted and then laid over the text. Another way to highlight text is to cut out small color arrows (complementary to the color of the label's background board) and lay them next to the text to be highlighted. Never use highlighter pen.

- Cases should not be overly full.

STEP SIX
Prepare Publicity

Once the exhibit is planned, a news release about the exhibit should be sent to a variety of media. (Chapter 1 in this book provides guidelines on preparing and distributing news releases.) If possible, the release should be sent at least two to four weeks before the exhibit opening. After the exhbit opens, a photo can be sent with an additional news release in which the ongoing success of the exhibit is detailed.

STEP SEVEN
Evaluate the Exhibits Program

Evaluation should examine the entire exhibits program as well as the individual exhibits and displays that make up the program. Questions that might be asked include:

- Are the exhibits and displays meeting the criteria set forth in the Exhibits Policy?

- Is the informal (word of mouth) feedback about the exhibits positive?

- Are additional suggestions for other exhibits being received?

- Are any of the exhibits being picked up by the local media for a news article or broadcast comments?

- In what ways can the program be improved?

- Is it worth having an exhibits/display program?

To get answers to these questions, librarians must be vigilant. It helps to have a notebook where comments are recorded, and, if time and staff are available, a short survey can be handed out to people after they have viewed the exhibit.

SOURCES OF ADDITIONAL INFORMATION

American Library Association. Exhibit Spaces and Bulletin Boards: An Interpretation of the LIBRARY BILL OF RIGHTS. Chicago: American Library Association, 1991.

Included here are guidelines for ensuring that exhibits and bulletin boards conform to standards of intellectual freedom as they are outlined in the LIBRARY BILL OF RIGHTS, articles I, II, and VI.

Association of College and Research Libraries, Systems and Procedures Exchange. *Exhibits in ARL Libraries.* Washington, D.C.: ARL, 1986.

The Association of Research Libraries surveyed its members in mid–1985 concerning staffing, administration, and local issues regarding the mounting of exhibits. Of the 70 members responding, 46 supplied documents. Included in this volume are sample policies and procedures, planning materials, job descriptions, facilities information, and publicity materials.

Borgwardt, Stephanie. *Library Display.* 2nd ed. Johannesburg: Witwatersrand University Press, 1970.

The author discusses the theory of library display (definition, purposes and objectives, subject selection, and various exhibits), practical aspects of displays (including types of displays, lettering, slogans, publicity, and reading lists), and children's library displays.

Casterline, Gail Farr. *Archives and Manuscripts: Exhibits.* Chicago: Society of American Archivists, 1980.

Chapters address issues relevant to the display of archival and manuscript materials, including the planning and development of displays; conservation and security of display materials; design and technique; program coordination; and administrative considerations, including funding, lending materials for exhibit, insurance, evaluation, and record keeping.

Coplan, Kate. *Effective Library Exhibits: How to Prepare and Promote Good Displays.* 2nd ed. Dobbs Ferry, N.Y.: Oceana Publications, 1974.

Chapters cover the case for exhibits; display ideas and arrangements; preparation and techniques; posters, signs, and showcards; tips for teachers; library book fairs; lighting; promotion; and silk screen. The diversified display suggestions chapter presents photos of over 90 displays and exhibits.

Everhart, Nancy, Claire Hartz, and William Kreiger. *Library Displays.* Metuchen, N.J.: Scarecrow Press, 1989.

The introduction to this resource discusses types of displays, ways to identify ideas, how to gather materials, and how to plan for displays. Section one presents 39 displays with photographs and lists of materials; section two presents other display ideas; and section three describes materials and techniques.

Garvey, Mona. *Library Displays: Their Purpose, Construction and Use.* New York: H.W. Wilson Company, 1969.

This well-illustrated resource discusses the value of displays; design, planning, lettering, and illustrations for displays; and specific ideas for displays.

Kohn, Rita. *Experiencing Displays.* Metuchen, N.J.: Scarecrow Press, 1982.

Kohn provides a variety of creative display ideas and a basic means for implementing them. Also included is a glossary of display terms.

Schaeffer, Mark. *Library Displays Handbook.* New York: H.W. Wilson, 1991.

Part one of this down-to-earth resource provides information on techniques and materials; part two provides suggestions for applying the techniques described in part one; and part three describes the production of specific types of displays. Kohn also provides a list of sources for display materials, suggestions for appropriate computer software, lists of additional readings, a monthly almanac of display themes, and generic display templates.

Whole Person Catalog. Chicago: American Library Association, n.d.

Available from the Director of Public Programs (American Library Association), this is a 21-page guide to humanities-oriented reading and discussion programs and exhibitions offered by libraries and nonprofit organizations throughout the United States. It lists approximately 100 discussion themes, as well as exhibits available from various organizations. The *Whole Person News* provides updates on exhibits and how libraries are using them.

Library Publications

What if you hold the world's best program and nobody comes? As new services and programs are developed by library staff, the need to make the public aware of these services and programs grows. A variety of publicity methods can be used to publicize these events. The following publication formats can help publicize the world's best programs.

WHAT IS A LIBRARY PUBLICATION?

The purpose of a library-produced publication is to directly communicate a specific message to a specific audience. The types of publications that a library most commonly produces include:

Newsletters

Newsletters are regularly published informational resources which provide relevant information about the library at periodic intervals. Newsletters are printed on both sides of a page, and generally measure 8-1/2″ × 11″. Depending upon the money available, newsletters range in length from two sides of one page to many pages.

Brochures

Brochures are two-sided, half-fold or tri-fold publications which inform the public about a library's ongoing services.

Flyers

Flyers are one-sided full or half sheets which publicize a one-time library program or a series of related library programs.

Posters

Posters are one-sided sheets which generally range in size from 8-1/2″ × 11″ to 8-1/2″ × 14″ to 11″ × 17″. Posters are printed on heavy paper, and are posted to advertise one-time library programs or a series of related library programs.

Bookmarks

Bookmarks are small promotional devices which provide information about the ongoing programs or services of a library. Some of the more popular informational items for a bookmark include booklists, library policies, addresses of legislators, calendars of events, and seasonal themes.

CREATING A PUBLICATION

In order to design an effective publication, the following steps should be taken.

STEP ONE
Define the Purpose of the Publication

Each type of publication that the library produces should have a written statement in which the goals and objectives of the publication are outlined. The purpose statement should also describe the ways in which the proposed publication will achieve the stated goals and objectives.

STEP TWO
Adopt an Editorial Policy

A written editorial policy for each type of publication that the library produces will avoid confusion as the publication is produced. The editorial policy should:

- Specify who is responsible for writing, editing, and overseeing production. Although many people will be involved in the production of a library publication, one person should be in charge as editor.

- Specify the writing style to be used for the publication. The purpose of the publication will usually determine the writing style. For example, a newsletter for young adults might use a casual style, but a newsletter for business leaders in the community will probably use a more formal style of writing.

- Specify the format of the publication. The elements of format include considerations such as the publication's logo, design of the masthead, page layout and design, ink color, artwork, typeface selection, and paper.

STEP THREE
Establish a Budget

The amount of money that is available for the production of a library publication affects all aspects of the project. Specifically, the budget determines:

- frequency of publication or revision

- length of the publication and number of copies printed

- whether pictures will be used

- whether color will be used, and how many colors will be used

- who will publish the final product (e.g., the library or a commercial publisher)

- how the final product will be published (e.g., typeset, printed, or photocopied)

- how the final product will be distributed

STEP FOUR
Establish Distribution Mechanisms

Depending upon the amount of money that is available, and depending upon the type of distribution which is deemed most effective for achieving the purpose of the publication, various distribution mechanisms may be used. The easiest, but most expensive, is to hire a professional mailing service to mail the publication directly to individuals. Less expensive, but more labor intensive, is to use the library's mailing lists for a bulk mailing which the library staff prepares. The least expensive distribution method, but not necessarily the most effective, is informal distribution of the publication from the library's circulation desk or other public outlets (e.g., grocery stores, Welcome Wagon organizations, Realtors, Chambers of Commerce).

STEP FIVE
Establish a General Layout for the Publication

All library publications should incorporate principles of good design in which a balance is maintained between creative expression and practical consideration of available resources. Laying out a publication is not an exact science, but there are some elements that need to be considered:

Proportion

Proportion concerns the size relationships of the elements in the layout. Everything that is included in the publication should be proportionate to everything else. Generally, symmetrical proportions are less interesting than nonsymmetrical proportions. Figure 3.1 provides an example of a nonsymmetrical layout for a newsletter page.

FIGURE 3.1 Sample Newsletter Nonsymmetrical Layout

MY MASTHEAD

Month or Season, Year   Issue & Volume Number

Name of sponsoring organization   (12 point sans serif type)   Slogan or statement of purpose

This is a 24 point Helvetica headline

Major stories usually have 24 point bold sans serif (Helvetica) headline. Secondary stories usually have 18 point headlines. Fillers and personal notes generally use 14 point.

Use upper and lower case when writing headlines. Capitalize the first word. All other words, except proper nouns, will be in lowercase letters.

Use 10 point serif type (Times) with 2 points of leading for the body of the article.

Use 6 points of leading between paragraphs with no indents.

Format will be 8-1/2″ × 11″.

The 3-column grid will be 13-1/2 picas wide with 1-1/2 pica alleys.

Subheads in 12 point bold sans serif

Allow 20 points of leading above the subhead and 6 points of leading below.

Stories can end with a small square or dingbat. ■ ◀

Photos can be 1, 2, or 3 columns wide.

Captions will be in 12 point bold serif type with 2 points of leading (12/14). Placement will be below the photograph or illustration.

Secondary stories will have 18 point sans serif bold headlines

The body of the article can have justified edges or can be uneven.

Place page numbers consistently throughout the publication in 10 point serif type.

A border, 1/2″ from all but the top edge of the page can help to give a finished look to the newsletter. ■

INSIDE . .

- **INSIDE heading will be 12 point bold sans serif type.**

- **Listings will be in 10 point serif type bold with 6 points of leading between each.**

Once you've filled in the newsletter specifications sheet you can make a visual specifications sheet like this one. It not only allows you to read the specs, but to see them as well.

Dominance

Dominance concerns the emphasis that a publication gives to one element in order to make it stand out. Dominance can be achieved through the effective use of size, color, texture, or shape.

Balance

Balance concerns the arrangement of the elements in a publication. For example, a symmetrical (formal) balance creates a classic look which denotes dignity, dependability, strength, stability, and sincerity. In this type of balance, everything on the page uniformly emanates from the center. In contrast, an asymmetrical (informal) balance creates a relaxed and free look. In this type of balance, everything on the page is arranged at different distances from the center.

Flow

The flow of a publication should create a sense of order in which a person's eye is led from one element to another, hopefully in the order of their importance. For example, a headline should lead the eye to illustrations, which, in turn, should lead the eye to written copy that identifies the library or library event. It is traditional to lead the eye from the upper left of the page to the lower right. Figures 3.2a, 3.2b, and 3.2c provide some sample layouts for promotional text.

Contrast

Contrast in a publication creates excitement and tension. Contrast may include horizontal and vertical positioning of elements; light and dark lines; large and small letters; negative and positive backgrounds; thick and thin lines; geometric shapes and loose, flowing shapes; and bold or light type. Illustrations can also be used to provide contrast. Figure 3.3 provides an example of how to use various contrast elements on a printed page.

Unity

Unity refers to how well the layout of a publication works overall. All elements in the publication must work in harmony. To establish unity, layouts can contain overlapped elements or shapes, or background colors, borders, boxes, and lines that are repeated. Effective use of white space also creates unity. Figure 3.3 provides an example of how to use various unity elements on a printed page.

FIGURE 3.2a **Sample Layouts—Simple Styles**

If your newsletter . . .

- is mainly text

- has a short production time

If you . . .

- have limited graphic design skill

- have other tasks as well as production of a newsletter

These styles work for you!

1-column grid

Scholar's margin grid #1

FIGURE 3.2b   Sample Layouts—Intermediate Styles

If your newsletter . . .

• is mostly text

• has only one to three photos or pieces of art per issue

If you . . .

• have limited graphic design equipment or beginning graphic design experience

These styles work for you!

2-column grid

Scholar's margin grid #2

FIGURE 3.2c   Sample Layouts—Advanced Styles

If your newsletter . . .

- has long and short articles

- is full of photos, art work, charts

If you . . .

- have solid graphic design skills

- have sufficient time and/or production help

These styles work for you!

3-column grids

FIGURE 3.3   For Visual Interest Add . . .

Graphic Device	Good	Use Sparingly	Function
Lines ☰	X		• Organizes articles • Enhances readability
Boxes ☐	X		• Organizes articles • Enhances readability
Fancy Borders		X	• Can direct the eye and fills white space.
REVERSE		X	• Grabs attention but drops readability by 50%
❝ Lift and enlarge quotes from text of article ❞	X		• Attracts the eye • Breaks up copy but use only one per page
Subheads Subheads	X		• Breaks up copy • Enhances readability
Charts 📈	X		• Good visual information method
Screens		X	• Attracts reader • Make sure type is readable over screen
Clip Art ☀	X		• Attracts the eye • Enhances content • Adds informality
White Space	X		• Attracts the eye • Breaks up text • Makes text more readable
Fillers/ In-house Promos Your Name Here	X		• Informs quickly • Adds variety to "lists" pages

STEP SIX
Evaluation of Publication

In order to determine whether or not the publicity campaign was success, the publication methods need to be evaluated. The following questions could be used for this evaluative process:

- Did the publication meet the goals and objectives?

- Did the publication reach the targeted audience?

- Was the publication within budget?

- Can this publication be used again?

- Did the publication display elements of good design?

- Was the selected format appropriate for the occasion?

In the case of newsletters all of the above evaluative questions can be used including:

- Was the editorial policy effective?

- Was the writing style appropriate for the targeted audience?

- Was the format and design of the newsletter effective?

If the evaluation process finds that the publication did not meet the purpose for which it was created, the above elements can be used to suggest modification for future projects.

SOURCES OF ADDITIONAL INFORMATION

Beach, Mark. *Designing Your Newsletter.* Manzanita, Ore.: Elk Ridge Publishing, 1994.

Newsletter format, design, and layout are illustrated in this publication. Examples of one-, two-, or three-column newsletters are shown, the advantages and disadvantages of each are described, and examples of nameplates, mastheads, calendars, and photo layouts are provided.

Floyd, Elaine. *Marketing with Newsletters.* New Orleans: EF Communications, 1991.

The author is president of EF Communications, a newsletter writing and production service that has developed over 50 newsletters for many types of organizations. This book is divided into four parts that correspond with the acronym RISE—Recognition, Image, Specifics, and Enactment. The first two chapters provide good basic information about marketing and newsletters, and the chapters about design, writing, and layout techniques are especially helpful.

Parker, Roger C. *Looking Good in Print.* 3rd ed. Chapel Hill, N.C.: Ventana Press, 1993.

Designed for use by desktop publishers with little or no graphic design background, this book outlines the skills necessary to create attractive, effective printed materials. There are numerous examples of newsletters, advertisements, brochures, and manuals. The book will provide novice desktop publishers with many ideas, and the "Getting Down to Business" section is a must read.

Siegle, Toni. "Principles of Design." *Clip Bits.* Peoria, Ill.: Dynamic Graphics, Inc. May 1992.

Siegle outlines six elements of design in this article, and demonstrates each element with advertising examples.

Planning Special Events

A special event is an event that will be held just once and is focused on a special purpose. Special events may be focused on attracting either loyal or new audiences, or both. Some examples of special events which are created to celebrate a specific chapter in an institution's development might include a groundbreaking ceremony, a building dedication, or an anniversary celebration. Special events may also be created for other types of targeted purposes. For example, a library might host a job fair, awards banquet, or a logo contest. Special events are different from "programs" in that, unlike the one-time special event, programs are defined as regularly booked and continuing events. Some examples of programs are lecture series, book discussion groups, movie series, summer reading clubs, and story hours. This chapter deals with planning a special event, or a one-time event which is focused on a specific purpose.

CREATING A SPECIAL EVENT

The following steps will ensure a successful special event.

STEP ONE
Develop Strategies for Success

- Make sure that the purpose for the special event is important enough to merit the time and expense that will be necessary in order to stage, publicize, and evaluate the event.

- Carefully match the type of event that is selected to the purpose that it serves.

- Ensure that the library staff fully supports the special event.

- Determine special groups that may have a stake in the event so that the special event's total attendance potential can be realized. Special groups to target might include library patrons, local politicians, business leaders, senior citizens, and ethnic populations.

- Start the planning at least three months, and in many cases, one year, ahead of time.

- Develop ways in which to evaluate the event's success. Measurable event objectives might include attendance, the amount of money raised, the number of new library cards issued, or increases in circulation of materials.

- Talk to other librarians who have successfully staged similar events.

STEP TWO
Develop a Checklist

A checklist provides a step-by-step guide to organizing and executing a special event. Figure 4.1 is an example of a checklist for an open house special event.

STEP THREE
Create the Budget

The objective of an event budget is to provide the event planners with a financial blueprint. The budget should be specific, and it should assume less revenue than expenses. The budget should include pre-event expenses (printing, permits, insurance); actual event costs (speakers, entertainers, food, supplies, security); and revenue opportunities (sponsorship, ticket sales, donations, concession sales).

STEP FOUR
Consider Logistics

There is no infallible formula for carrying out an event. With many activities often going on simultaneously, there are many details to be checked, and many chances for little things to go wrong. Major areas to consider for a smoothly coordinated event include the following:

- The space or spaces for the event must be appropriately large or small and should be well designed to accommodate all of the event's special needs.

- Utility support for the event and for the planning process must include electric, gas, water, lighting, and telephones. Support might also include special equipment such as photocopiers, computers, and computer printers.

- People in charge of setting up for the event should consider whether they will need setup of tables, chairs, tents, portable toilets, parking, security, first aid, information, sound, lights, and signage.

FIGURE 4.1 **Open House Checklist**

_____ Select chair and members of the Planning Committee.

_____ Planning Committee sets event date and develops master plan for the open house.

_____ Select chairs for each of the following subcommittees:

    _____ *Arrangements Subcommittee*
        Plans tour routes; prepares and sets up exhibits, displays, demonstrations.

    _____ *Hosts Subcommittee*
        Greets guests; handles registration; mingles with guests; distributes booklets, annual reports, and other related literature as guests arrive and leave.

    _____ *Tour Guides Subcommittee (One member for every ten guests)*
        Conducts tours, answers questions, keeps groups moving.

    _____ *Traffic and Safety Subcommittee*
        Prepares and posts signs, sets up and maintains checkroom, keeps elevators from becoming overloaded, keeps traffic moving smoothly in tours, provides security at selected tour points, enforces fire regulations, oversees parking.

    _____ *Invitations Subcommittee*
        Compiles master invitation list, designs the printed invitation, prepares letters of invitation for special guests, determines date for mailing invitations, determines date for collecting responses, sends out invitations, monitors responses.

    _____ *Refreshments Subcommittee*
        Purchases food and paper goods, sets up buffets and beverages, helps serve guests.

_____ Organize workers to serve on above committees.

_____ Hold a joint meeting of Planning Committee and subcommittees to explain Open House plan and its purpose.

_____ Formulate a publicity plan, including deadlines for media to be contacted.

_____ Prepare copy for printed program, including information about tour itinerary, brief facts about the library, names of its governing board, and names of the event's Planning Committee.

_____ Hold a "day before the event" briefing meeting. Distribute event schedule to each committee member, discuss what each person will be expected to do that day, and distribute identification badges.

_____ During Open House set up several registration tables and stagger tour schedules to avoid bottlenecks. Distribute event program as guests arrive, so that they know what to expect.

_____ After the Open House:

    _____ Mail printed program, together with appropriate letter and enclosure, to selected people who did not attend the event. For example, you might want to mail the printed program and a letter to people who received invitations but did not come.

    _____ Send photos to media, and to people pictured, thanking them for their participation.

    _____ Thank everyone who helped make the event successful.

    _____ Evaluate the Open House to determine how the next one could be improved.

- People in charge of cleaning up should consider how everything will be cleaned up and disposed of after the event and who will do it.

- Public service sectors must be made aware of the special event. These groups include, but are not limited to, police, fire, emergency medical services, and the department of public works.

- An emergency plan should be worked out for dealing with weather contingencies or other unforeseen circumstances.

- All of the people involved in the event's execution must be knowledgeable about their duties and must be provided with an entire event plan which includes emergency procedures.

- All of the people involved in the event's execution must know whether or not they will be paid for their services, how much, and when.

- Transportation needs must be carefully considered, with special attention paid to parking, mass transit, parking permits, special requests from disabled individuals, and transportation which might be necessary within the event facility, or between event locations.

STEP FIVE
Plan the Publicity

Selecting the right publicity vehicles to promote a special event takes creative thinking balanced with practicality. The primary objective for special event publicity is, obviously, to publicize the event. However, secondary objectives should also be considered. For example, should the publicity also:

- inform, educate, or entertain?

- increase awareness of or attendance at the event?

- build a base of support from a specific audience?

- facilitate good community relations?

Depending upon the objectives for the publicity, librarians will want to choose from the various publicity options that are discussed in the other chapters of this book. Aspects of publicity that should be carefully considered include the following:

- Develop a media plan. Here, the choices include:

    Print media (press releases and advertisements)

    Television (public service announcements and news coverage)

    Radio (public service announcements and talk shows)

    Direct mail that is targeted to existing and potential audiences. If direct mail is used, a tracking mechanism that will allow the librarians to evaluate the usefulness of this expensive publicity mechanism should be developed.

Specialty items (e.g., posters, flyers, bumper stickers, exhibits, billboards, balloons, envelope stuffers, banners, refrigerator magnets, postage meter imprints).

- Organize a guest list which comprises special guests who will receive VIP invitations (i.e., trustees; mayors; city/governing officials; heads of civic and fraternal organizations; business, professional, and education leaders; the media).

- Develop a plan for welcoming or seating special guests.

STEP SIX
Evaluate the Event

An effective way to evaluate a special event is to evaluate separately each of the parts that went into staging it: strategies, the checklist that was used, the budget, logistics, and the effectiveness of the publicity which was used. It is also most effective if evaluation occurs very soon after the event, so that details are still fresh in people's minds. In order to help evaluate an event, librarians might want to ask participants to fill out a short evaluative questionnaire before leaving, or they might want to record officially all informal comments which are made as participants leave. The people involved in staging the event should also be queried about the effectiveness of the processes that shaped and implemented the event, and one person, or a designated group of people, should write a final report which provides a troubleshooting checklist for future events.

Specific questions and observations that are used to evaluate the success of a special event should address general evaluative criteria, including:

- Did the event fulfill its original goals and objectives? If it did, the evaluators might want to analyze why the event was a success in order to use it as a model for future events. If the event did not fulfill its original goals and objectives, evaluators should determine why, and should develop strategies for improvement.

- What elements of the special event worked well and what elements needed further fine-tuning? For example, were the master invitation lists targeted well enough, or did the targeting process fall short; which vendors should be used again; how accurately were expenditures predicted; were there items missing on the checklist?

- Was the event well attended?

- Was informal and formal feedback about the event positive?

- Given all that went into staging the special event, was it worth doing?

Finally, it is very important to remember to celebrate your successes, and to thank all those responsible for contributing to an event's success.

SOURCES OF ADDITIONAL INFORMATION

Edsall, Marian S. *Library Promotion Handbook.* Phoenix, Ariz.: Oryx Press, 1980.

This "how-to" guide describes ways in which to use the tools of publicity and promotion in a library's public relations plan. The special events chapter includes a wealth of creative ideas gleaned from libraries across the country, including publicity flyers, an event planning checklist, typical and atypical events, anniversary and centennial themes, grand openings, and new building dedications.

Kotler, Philip and Alan R. Andreason. *Strategic Marketing for Nonprofit Organizations.* 4th ed. Englewood Cliffs, N.J.: Prentice-Hall, 1991.

While earlier editions of this book were designed to give an instructional overview of marketing principles, this edition contains much information from marketing practitioners. Included are checklists, practical hints, narratives of experiences, and sample materials from nonprofit organizations.

Sherman, Steve. *ABC's of Library Promotion.* Metuchen, N.J.: Scarecrow Press, 1992.

Included here are chapters devoted to creating special events for academic, school, and public libraries.

CHAPTER FIVE

ANN HAMILTON
with contributions by
SUSAN M. HILTON

Desktop Publishing and the Importance of Diversity and Image

DESKTOP COMPUTER SOFTWARE

A word processing package such as WordPerfect™,[1] or a desktop publishing package such Pagemaker™,[2] can be invaluable in creating public relations materials. Computer magazines are excellent sources to help you choose software best suited to your needs. A number of books are available that can help users to get the most out of their software packages. It is especially helpful to watch for good examples of public relations materials, and then ask the creators what software packages they used.

Librarians should find word processing or publishing software they like and keep it handy. Also, librarians should take advantage of classes about the software packages they use; many classes that teach the use of specific software packages are offered at libraries, or at local schools.

Once the basics of a software package have been mastered, it is possible to produce innovative and professional-looking printed resources. For example, you can:

- Create variety through careful use of different print styles and type sizes. Some printers also allow changes in appearance. The print styles may vary according to the printer used (See Figure 5.1). However, mixing too many print styles can obscure the message.

- Create interest by inserting topical or humorous graphics (See Figure 5.2). Word processing and desktop publishing software programs include graphics; desktop publishing can provide, with additional

---

1. WordPerfect is availble from WordPerfect Corporation, 1555 N. Technology Way, Orem, Utah 84057-2399, as well as from retailers and mail order houses.

2. Aldus Pagemaker for Windows (version 5.0a) is produced by Aldus Corporation, 411 First Ave., Seattle, WA 98104. It is available from retail outlets and mail order houses.

FIGURE 5.1   Mixing Too Many Type Styles

Mixing several print *styles* *can* obscure *your* *message*

Example created using WordPefect 5.1 and the font, size, and appearance choices available for a Hewlett-Packard LaserJet III printer.

FIGURE 5.2   Create Interest with Graphics

Create interest by inserting topical or humorous graphics.

Created with file **balloons.wpg** in WordPefect using the graphics feature and a Hewlett-Packard LaserJet III printer.

scanning and photo editing software, capability for printing photographs directly from the computer.

- Create standard forms for schedules and holdings locations, for newsletter templates, and for many other recurring publications. Forms can be stored and easily revised as information changes (See Figures 5.3 and 5.4).

FIGURE 5.3   **Standard Form: Making a Suggestion**

HOW TO MAKE A SUGGESTION

1. Log into the Library Catalog through one of the networked computers.

2. Type SUG at the >> prompt and press <enter>.

3. At the next screen type SUG and press <enter> again.

4. Follow the instructions on the SUGGESTION BOX screen.

We appreciate your suggestions. They are usually read daily during the week, and responses are posted as soon as possible. It is helpful to have your name so that we can contact you if you need personal assistance for an urgent question, or if we need to follow up on a suggestion or question that is not clear. However, anonymous suggestions are also appreciated.

If you have questions or comments about the library's suggestion system, please contact the Associate Director in the library's administrative office. Our phone number is 681-5115.

FIGURE 5.4   **Standard Form: Local History Quiz**

PENN STATE TRIVIA

What do you know about the Convention Site?

1.   What was the original name of the school that became known as the Pennsylvania State College in 1874? When was it founded?

2.   The creamery is part of what College? What is it famous for?

3.   What Penn State professor has been President of SCAP as well as Speaker of the Year? Extra points for the years.

4.   When was Old Main built? When was it rebuilt?

5.   Where is the Penn State Football Hall of Fame?

6.   Who painted the Land Grant Mural in Old Main?

7.   Name one Pittsburgh Steeler who played football for Joe Paterno and is in the NFL Hall of Fame?

8.   What Penn State professor has been chair of the Communication Department and the 1990 Speaker of the Year?

9.   Who has been ECA President, Executive Secretary of SCAP and the Director of the Pennsylvania High School Speech League?

10.   Who won the Heisman trophy from Penn State? In what year?

11.   How long has Joe Paterno been the Head Coach of the Nittany Lions?

12.   Where does the name Nittany Lions come from?

For the answers to this quiz, check further in the newsletter.

The Pennsylvania Communicator   *Speech Communication Association of Pennsylvania*

Created using an IBM-compatible personal computer and Aldus Pagemaker for Windows.

- Create folded brochures. For example, in WordPerfect, brochures can easily be created by setting the paper size to 11 × 8-1/2 (landscape) and using columns. For a trifold brochure, copy can be printed on both sides of the page with three columns of information per side (See Figure 5.5). A single-fold brochure can be created using the same technique to create two columns for each side of the paper.

Word processing software may provide all the computing power a library needs for publishing, especially if simple brochures and one-time public relations publications are being produced. Desktop publishing may be preferable if librarians are producing newsletters and other publications that use the same format each time; library publications that utilize many headings, subheadings, and indexes; or signs (i.e., changes of hours for holidays,

FIGURE 5.5   **Sample Trifold Brochure Design**

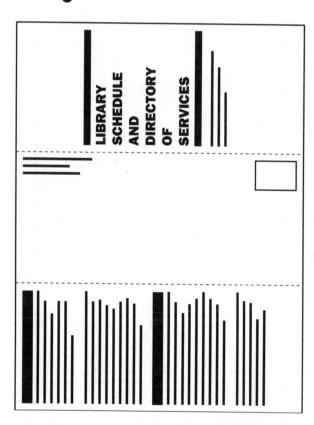

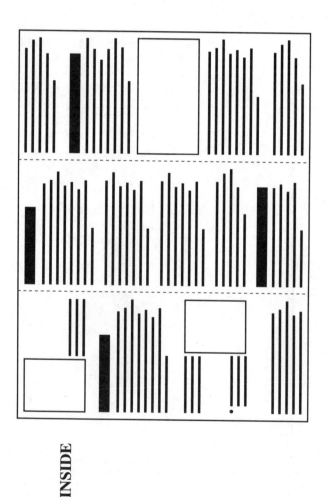

announcements of library events, directional signs). A good book to read before deciding on the most effective uses of desktop publishing might be Walt Crawford's *Desktop Publishing for Librarians* (Boston: G.K. Hall, 1990).

PHOTOCOPIERS

Brochures, flyers, posters, and other public relations materials can be reproduced easily and inexpensively on a photocopy machine. It is especially helpful if the photocopier can be used to enlarge or reduce copy. If that feature is available, the ability to cut and paste information and graphics to create attractive pieces is almost unlimited.

Some helpful hints to keep in mind:

- Use correcting fluid sparingly and with precision. This will keep the master copy and additional copies clean and professional looking.

- When the sheet being copied does not reach all areas of the copier plate, place another larger piece of paper behind that sheet to prevent lines from appearing on final copy.

- Enhance creative possibilities for a photocopy machine by maintaining a supply of paper in a variety of colors which will work with your particular photocopier. Use color to increase the effectiveness of the piece. If you want to attract attention, use a bright neon color. For a more subtle message, use a pastel.

- Keep at least a small supply of every size of paper that your photocopy machine will accept. The more choices available, the more flexibility you will have for tailoring your public relations materials to your specific needs.

PAYING ATTENTION TO DIVERSITY ISSUES

Library patrons are very diverse. It is important to keep that diversity in mind when planning and creating public relations materials. The diversity of the target audience should be considered throughout the creative process. Some questions to ask and some points to keep in mind include:

- Should the public relations effort appeal to men or women (boys or girls)? Or both?

- How tall is the target audience? Keep in mind that displays should not be too high or too low to be accessible to all members of the target audience.

- Should the public relations effort appeal to persons of different ages? If so, keep all of the potential age groups in mind. For example, do not use graphics that are targeted only at a small segment of the target audience.

- Should the public relations effort be produced in more than one language? If patrons include persons of a number of different nationalities, materials produced in different languages may be welcomed. This is particularly true of brochures describing library services and directional signs assisting patrons in locating materials. Care should be taken, however, in the use of multiple languages. Can a program be presented in more than one language? If not, care should be taken to insure that flyers advertising it do not imply that more than one language will be used.

- Are your public relations products accessible to persons with disabilities? Tactile displays, audio recordings, and braille copies of descriptive materials can assist persons with visual disabilities. Having a signer present during a program or providing printed texts of audio presentations can assist persons with hearing disabilities. Also, exhibits should be as accessible as possible to persons with physical disabilities.

- Have you avoided sexism in the language or graphics you used?

- Have you avoided stereotyping in the graphics or language you used? Not only are certain types of stereotyping illegal, but any library whose public relations efforts include stereotyped images or languages will alienate a large segment of its service area.

- Have you avoided ageism? Older adults are a respected part of the community, they can provide a wealth of information and advice for librarians, and they constitute a very powerful public relations tool. Library public relations should include older adults as an integral target audience.

CREATING A CONSISTENT IMAGE

Creating a consistent and professional image for your library's public relations materials is very important. For example, you create a better impression on patrons if you print signs on the same color paper and place them in holders than if you generate a lot of signs and flyers in different colors and attach them to every available surface.

Getting information to patrons is important, but the long-lasting effects of a poorly presented example of public relations can far outweigh urgency. Make time to think about issues of consistency in all public relations efforts.

A N D R E A   L.   M I L L E R

Public Relations Lessons from Business and Communications

. . . If the circus is coming to town and you paint a sign saying "Circus Coming to the Fairground Saturday," that's advertising. If you put the sign on the back of an elephant and walk him into town, that's promotion. If the elephant walks through the mayor's flower bed, that's publicity. And if you can get the mayor to laugh about it, that's public relations.

(Public Interest Public Relations, *Promoting Issues and Ideas,* 1)

T he purpose of this annotated bibliography is to provide a number of significant resources for librarians to use when planning a successful public relations campaign. A great deal of information can be learned from the experts in the fields of business, marketing, advertising, and communications, since these are the professionals who live and die by competitive public relations. It is their ads and slogans that jingle through consumers' heads as they shop at the supermarket and at department stores. These individuals inspire consumers to buy one kind of headache remedy over another; and if they can do all of that, they certainly should be able to tell librarians how to promote libraries and programs so that they are in the forefront of constituents' minds. Stopping by, and supporting, the local library can become just as easy, as natural, and as comfortable as choosing that peanut butter that is "more peanuttier" if public relations lessons are learned well.

Sources included were chosen on the basis of recent dates of publication; only books from 1980 to the present are listed. One source that is a literature review covers the decade of the seventies. Most of the titles listed are light on theory and heavy on practicality, and most of the ideas and suggestions that are presented can be implemented at low cost. Many of the listed titles are handbooks or workbooks that can be referred to again and again as the public relations plan is being developed, revised, and evaluated. Librarians may wish to obtain one copy of some of the listed titles for their library collections, and another to be used as a personal workbook. Some textbooks and reference books were included in order to have resources that covered the entire subject—from historical background to current procedures, media, and technology.

Examples and illustrations used in the listed titles to demonstrate concepts and ideas are primarily from business and the corporate world; however, the principles and plans are readily adaptable to the nonprofit world of the library. One note of regret: those titles that did discuss realms other than business such as charities, community service clubs and organizations, public education, and colleges, never mentioned libraries—of any kind. Libraries' conspicuous absence truly points out the need for practitioners to recognize the vitality and power of public relations and plan programs that give libraries a higher profile.

SELECTED ANNOTATED BIBLIOGRAPHY

Baker, Kim, and Sunny Baker. *How to Promote, Publicize, and Advertise Your Growing Business: Getting the Word Out without Spending a Fortune.* New York: John Wiley & Sons, Inc., 1992.

After working for more than fifteen years in advertising, Kim and Sunny Baker recognized that all groups need to promote and publicize to stay viable. This "how-to" book is a practical guide to using marketing communications tools to meet the specific needs of any group. The authors first recommendation is to identify clearly the audience that one wishes to reach and then determine the message that will appeal to that particular audience. This suggestion is one that is familiar to librarians and is a comfortable means of edging into the "business" of advertising. The process of developing an advertising program is taken step-by-step. Also included are suggestions for advertising in the various media, for producing a quality news release, for organizing special events, and for saving money when there just isn't enough. Written in an easy-to-read style, this well indexed book could be used as a publicity workbook.

Beals, Melba. *Expose Yourself: Using the Power of Public Relations to Promote Your Business and Yourself.* San Francisco: Chronicle Books, 1990.

Beals opens her book with her own account of being thrust into the forefront of publicity when she was one of the first black children to be integrated into Little Rock's schools. Her story also became a top national news story, and today, after college and many years of work experience with the media and as a publicist with an impressive list of clients, she shares her insights into the necessity of promotional activity. This book takes readers step-by-step through the process of becoming one's own publicist and contains a chapter devoted to promoting non-profit organizations such as libraries. Another chapter of particular interest is a guide to creating events that present free promotional opportunities. The author's education and experience in journalism offer the reader special insight into handling the media.

Bly, Robert W. *Targeted Public Relations: How to Get Thousands of Dollars of Free Publicity for Your Product, Service, Organization, or Idea.* New York: Henry Holt and Company, 1993.

Recognizing that money for operational costs may leave little or nothing available for public relations, Robert Bly, copywriter and veteran marketing consultant, suggests that an organization can get more effec-tive, measurable results through the use of targeted public relations rather than through the use of direct mail or print advertising, which target the mass media. The specifics of his program seem exceptionally good for libraries since money is always tight (Bly's promotions are under $500.00) and librarians usually know, or can ascertain, the exact audi-ence that they wish to target. A promotion that is unique to Bly is that of "Selling Through Education" (reaching a more intelligent, savvy client through seminars, demonstrations, and teaching), something that is commonplace in any library. Also included in this well-indexed resource are writing tips common in other public relations handbooks.

Brown, Lillian. *Your Public Best: The Complete Guide to Making Successful Public Appearances in the Meeting Room, on the Platform, and on TV.* New York: Newmarket Press, 1989.

Lillian Brown has been chief makeup artist for CBS News and has also served in the same capacity during several Presidents' terms. It would be difficult to imagine an individual or organizational manager who could successfully lead his or her group into positive public relations without presenting the appropriate personal image. Brown's book is one that all professionals should read, follow, and refer to as one adds to a wardrobe. Topics covered include professional clothing, makeup, voice and public speaking, and making public appearances.

Hausman, Carl, and Philip Benoit. *Positive Public Relations.* 2nd edition. Blue Ridge Summit, Pa.: Liberty Hall Press, 1990.

This would serve well as a textbook or as a training manual for a beginner in public relations. Each step is carefully discussed, beginning with a definition of public relations and continuing with explanations of the workings of each medium. The unique feature of this text lies in its coverage of photography and production, including desktop publishing. It would be useful as a well-indexed reference source for individuals who are learning about public relations.

Heath, Robert L., and Richard Alan Nelson. *Issues Management: Corporate Public Policymaking in an Information Society.* Beverly Hills: SAGE Publications, Inc., 1985.

Doctors Heath and Nelson, professors of communication, collaborated to write about a topic that they believe to be more timely than "publicity" or "public relations." They indicate that a careful monitoring and study of issues management will place an organization in its community or in the marketplace more effectively than public relations will. Issues management attempts to identify and monitor trends in public opinion. In time, these trends may become public policy; thus, organizations need to be in tune to reflect this policy in "corporate codes of social responsibility." Their philosophy requires that issues management professionals keep a finger on the pulse of their constituencies at all times. When successful, issues management prevents damaging media coverage from occurring and institutes more rigorous organizational standards and behavior. Issues management is not for the casual reader, but the authors do make some points that should be considered as complementary to public relations.

Hill, Dennis Cole. *Power PR: A Streetfighter's Handbook to Winning Public Relations.* Hollywood, Fla.: Fell Publishers, Inc., 1990.

Hill, former editor-in-chief of *Business Quarterly of Colorado* and public relations coordinator for Nova Technological Center, presents advice for the practice of professional public relations, regardless of the type or size of business or organization. The key is getting the organizational name out into the marketing arena and into potential clients' minds. Corporate examples are used to clarify Hill's descriptions of the process. The majority of the text is devoted to the topic of dealing with the press, writing press releases, and holding press conferences. An appendix has examples of press releases and newsletters.

Levine, Michael. *Guerrilla P.R.: How You Can Wage an Effective Publicity Campaign . . . without Going Broke.* New York: HarperBusiness, 1993.

As the head of a major public relations firm in Hollywood, Levine knows well the importance of jungle fighting. However, in the book's foreword, written by Melvin Belli, Levine is characterized as a "superb teacher" who stops well before reaching ethical boundaries. The foundation of the author's technique lies in resourcefulness; individuals or groups who do not have monetary resources must make up for it with "moxie." The author also speaks about the importance of being passionate in public relations endeavors. Of course, one must first believe in oneself before anyone else will listen and believe. The book is self-proclaimed to be a publicity manifesto that will teach readers how to think like publicists. Each chapter has activities to practice principles just discussed, and examples are frequently used to illustrate the author's ideas. Most readers will want to refer to this book many times after the initial reading and practice.

Mercer, Laurie, and Jennifer Singer. *Opportunity Knocks: USING PR.* Radnor, Pa.: Chilton Book Company, 1989.

Much of the content of this book has been adequately covered by other titles included in this bibliography; however, Mercer and Singer devote several chapters to particularly difficult issues—dealing with crises and bad press. Following their advice can turn a bad experience around and help to recoup major losses. Their final note addresses the issue of working with other professionals such as typesetters, photographers, graphic artists, printers, and others. It is important to know what to expect from them as well as what an individual can demand of them.

Phillips, Charles S. *Secrets of Successful Public Relations: An Insider's Guide to the Strategies and Techniques That Work Today.* Englewood Cliffs, N.J.: Prentice-Hall, Inc., 1985.

Through many years of working as a practitioner of public relations, the author has developed a keen insight for practical approaches to the profession. The well-indexed text contains some elements found in other books included in this bibliography, but its most interesting chapters concern conducting internal and external communications audits and the qualitative research that follows the audits. Phillips takes readers through an audit process that enables auditors to see the organization as specific audience groups see it. He includes approaches to take, questions to ask, and interviewer personality traits. The external audit includes questioning visitors at the local tavern, attendees at community club meetings, the press, and any other community groups that might provide relevant information. A sample audit script is included. The research continues with employee attitude surveys (sample included) and administration of questionnaires to measure consumer product use. An example is presented for measuring the effectiveness of the house organ, or vehicle of communication for the organization.

Pinsdorf, Marion K. *Communicating When Your Company Is Under Siege: Surviving Public Crisis.* Lexington, Mass.: Lexington Books, 1987.

The time to deal with crisis is long before the crisis ever occurs. Pinsdorf uses corporate case histories to illustrate how one can survive trying times by having an understanding of the media and their needs, by presenting a genuine image of the organization, and by planning for the unexpected—good or bad. The author maintains that an organization can overcome scandal, rumors, and disasters through communication. Some of the interesting cases covered are Cabbage Patch Kids Fever, the Union Carbide tragedy at Bhopal, the Challenger explosion, and Love Canal. An extensive bibliography is included.

Public Interest Public Relations. *Promoting Issues & Ideas: A Guide to Public Relations for Nonprofit Organizations.* New York: The Foundation Center, 1987.

Public Interest Public Relations (PIPR) is a national communications firm that focuses on promoting issues and ideas for nonprofit organizations. This book does not require librarians to read between the lines and attempt to apply what big businesses do to smaller nonprofit groups. PIPR has heard all of the comments from nonprofit groups—"We're too small to get involved with PR"; "Our services will sell themselves"; and, "Everyone knows that we exist." PIPR demonstrates that most ideas such as these are just myths and get in the way of building public support, increasing membership, or promoting an event. The text of the book demonstrates how to build a public relations plan and presents plenty of examples for illustration. In fact, as the writers move through developing materials to support the public relations plan and into ways to garner publicity, the text is replete with illustrative releases, designs, and letters. Topics unique to this source include ways to lobby effectively and suggestions for dealing with new communications technologies. Directories of print publicity sources and broadcasting resources are included in an appendix. Other appendices include names and addresses of commercial public relations services, a glossary of terms, a public relations bibliography, and newsletter resources.

Ramacitti, David F. *Do-It-Yourself Publicity.* New York: AMACOM, 1990.

The purpose of this well-indexed book is to familiarize readers with the basics of publicity and assist them in writing their own publicity plan. The intended audience is individuals or organizations who do not have a professional public relations person on staff and who do not have the resources to hire an agency. This includes nonprofit organizations, support agencies, and clubs. The author assumes that the do-it-yourselfer will mostly be working with small-town, local media, so this book would be especially good for libraries in smaller settings. Ramacitti assists the reader in building a media contact file that is often vital in getting a foot in the door to a local television or radio station. A short bibliography and a complete glossary are included in appendices.

Reilly, Robert T. *Public Relations in Action.* 2nd edition. Englewood Cliffs, N.J.: Prentice-Hall, Inc., 1987.

Reilly, a professor of communications at the University of Nebraska at Omaha, has written an excellent textbook and reference source for the study of public relations. He includes background, theory, and research, and assists readers through the process of decision making and planning. He devotes space to writing for publicity and to production. An especially interesting and helpful section discusses financial public relations which prepares readers to release financial information from their organization to public scrutiny. Each chapter concludes with suggestions for further reading, exercises for practice, and case problems for further study and discussion. An appendix contains the Code of Professional Standards for the Public Relations Society of America.

Rein, Irving, Philip Kotler, and Martin R. Stoller. *High Visibility*. New York: Dodd, Mead & Company, 1987.

The purpose of *High Visibility* is to illustrate how celebrities came to be in elevated status and to demonstrate how readers might also rise to the same status. If one considers that the high visibility of library directors and staff can positively impact the library's image and its degree of public support, then one might also consider reading this text to gain personal and professional information to see how the task can be accomplished. The book is interesting and is peppered with celebrities' stories that add to the readability.

Roach, William J. *Planning in Public Relations and Organizational Communications: A Literature Review.* San Francisco: International Association of Business Communicators Foundation, 1984.

This resource is an extensive annotated bibliography of a search conducted in the public relations literature from 1974–84. No planning resources *per se* were included, but management titles on planning were. Periodicals, pamphlets, and reports were also included for a total of over 460 references. This resource may be helpful for the decade that this bibliography does not cover.

Saffir, Leonard. *Power Public Relations: How to Get PR to Work for You.* Lincolnwood, Ill.: NTC Business Books, 1992.

Saffir and his assistant, John Tarrant, both public relations executives, define public relations as something very much apart from advertising and as something that can replace it. They believe that to be successful in using advertising, clients must spend an inordinate amount of money; however, with public relations, clients have "massive strength and wide versatility" that is not so costly. The writers discuss important concepts such as public relations making the public want something; public relations offering feedback from the public to the client; and public relations as an important strategic weapon. Also included are tips on evaluating a public relations program and handling the press. Not a handbook or workbook, this is worthwhile reading based on its premise.

Schmertz, Herb. *Good-bye to the Low Profile: The Art of Creative Confrontation.* Boston: Little, Brown and Company, 1986.

Writing in an enjoyable style, Schmertz advises all readers who must face someone else in a confrontation to face the press, and to create their own distinctive personality. This book could also be used in any management class; however, most classroom reading is not this enjoyable. The author recognizes the difficulty that a manager or corporate representative faces when dealing with a "tough guy," or damaging rumors, or even a powerful political figure. His suggestions are sound and offer readers an opportunity to grow.

Smith, Jeanette. *The Publicity Kit: A Complete Guide for Entrepreneurs, Small Businesses, and Nonprofit Organizations.* New York: John Wiley & Sons, Inc., 1991.

The author's background as a communications specialist and public relations professional affords the novice reader an excellent opportunity to learn about the public relations process as well as the major role that newspapers play in enhancing a group's image. She spends time with readers who appreciate a little spoon-feeding to explain the styles of writing that newspapers look for, how to be successful in writing stories about group events, and how to establish good relations with the media. Five appendices provide samples of news releases; guidelines for photos; suggestions for writing goals and objectives for public relations; steps to use brainstorming successfully; and an annotated list of directories, style manuals, clipping bureaus, and nonprofit assistance. Also included are a glossary of terms for beginners and an index.

Paula Banks is the Public Information Officer of the Medina (Ohio) County District Library system. Banks is responsible for all aspects of public relations for the system, including producing news releases, creating and editing newsletters, and developing marketing displays. She has worked in libraries for four years.

William Buchanan is assistant professor of library science at Clarion University of Pennsylvania, Department of Library Science. Before coming to librarianship, Buchanan worked as the director of public information for a large nonprofit agency, and has also worked as a newspaper reporter and feature writer.

Dorothy Christiansen is currently Head of Special Collections and Archives, University Libraries, University at Albany, State University of New York (SUNY). She serves as editor of the SUNY Libraries' newsletter, *Library Update,* chairs the SUNY Libraries' Exhibits Committee, and has an ongoing involvement in the Libraries' public relations and exhibits program.

Ann Hamilton is Associate University Librarian at Georgia Southern University (Statesboro). She has been active in the LAMA Public Relations Section for six years. She is also active in the public relations activities of associations at state and regional levels.

Susan M. Hilton is assistant professor of communication at Clarion University of Pennsylvania, Department of Communication. She is editor of several professional newsletters and works extensively with desktop publishing and other publishing ventures.

Rashelle S. Karp is professor of library science at Clarion University of Pennsylvania, Department of Library Science. She is an active editor of books and journal articles, has published extensively in areas of interest to public librarians, and is a member of several publication committees of the American Library Association.

Debora Meskauskas is Public Information Officer of the Arlington Heights Memorial Library (Illinois), and is responsible for planning and budgeting the library's public information program directed to the 75,462 tax-supporting residents of Arlington Heights. The Public Information Office manages all library publications and graphics, and acts as spokesperson in representing the library to print and broadcast media. Meskauskas has worked as a public relations practitioner in hospitals and in public relations firms in Chicago, Cleveland, and Florida.

Andrea L. Miller is instructor of library science at Clarion University of Pennsylvania, Department of Library Science. She is a reviewer for *The Book Report,* has experience as a school librarian, and teaches in the areas of library administration and media and nonbook resources for libraries.